D1558609

I Love My Pet
Potbellied Pig

Aaron Carr

www.av2books.com

LET'S READ
AV²
BY WEIGL™
ADDED VALUE • AUDIO VISUAL

Go to **www.av2books.com**, and enter this book's unique code.

BOOK CODE

E 9 7 8 0 6 7

AV² by Weigl brings you media enhanced books that support active learning.

AV² provides enriched content that supplements and complements this book. Weigl's AV² books strive to create inspired learning and engage young minds in a total learning experience.

Your AV² Media Enhanced books come alive with...

Audio
Listen to sections of the book read aloud.

Video
Watch informative video clips.

Embedded Weblinks
Gain additional information for research.

Try This!
Complete activities and hands-on experiments.

Key Words
Study vocabulary, and complete a matching word activity.

Quizzes
Test your knowledge.

Slide Show
View images and captions, and prepare a presentation.

...and much, much more!

Published by AV² by Weigl
350 5th Avenue, 59th Floor New York, NY 10118
Website: www.av2books.com www.weigl.com

Library of Congress Cataloguing in Publication data available upon request.
Fax 1-866-449-3445 for the attention of the Publishing Records department.

ISBN 978-1-62127-296-0 (hardcover)
ISBN 978-1-62127-303-5 (softcover)

Printed in the United States of America in North Mankato, Minnesota
1 2 3 4 5 6 7 8 9 0 16 15 14 13 12

122012
WEP301112

Senior Editor: Aaron Carr   Art Director: Terry Paulhus

Weigl acknowledges Getty Images as the primary image supplier for this title. Cover: Bart van den Ordel.

I Love My Pet

Potbellied Pig

CONTENTS

3

I love my pet potbellied pig.
I take good care of her.

4

My pet potbellied pig was a piglet. She had to stay with her mother until she was six weeks old.

7

My pet potbellied pig was full grown after six months. She is about the size of a dog.

Potbellied pigs can weigh up to 200 pounds.

10

My pet potbellied pig
has a very big belly.
Her belly touches the ground.

My pet potbellied pig
needs to eat twice each day.
It is my job to make sure
she gets the right amount of food.

Potbellied pigs
will keep eating
until all of their food
is gone.

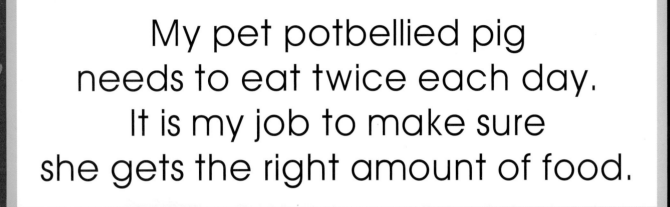

My pet potbellied pig sleeps on her own bed. She also has her own litter box.

My pet potbellied pig
likes to be very clean.
It is my job to bathe her,
brush her, and clean her teeth.

Potbellied pigs
need to wear sunscreen
on sunny days.

20

I make sure my pet potbellied pig is healthy.
I love my pet potbellied pig.

POTBELLIED PIG FACTS

These pages provide more detail about the interesting facts found in the book. They are intended to be used by adults as a learning support to help young readers round out their knowledge of each animal featured in the *I Love My Pet* series.

Pages 4–5

I love my pet potbellied pig. I take good care of her. Potbellied pigs are a type of miniature pig. They are about one-eighth the size of farm pigs. Potbellied pigs make excellent pets. They are clean, smart, playful, and easy to train. However, some cities have laws against keeping pigs as pets. Be sure to check the laws in your town or city before bringing home a pet potbellied pig.

Pages 6–7

My pet potbellied pig was a piglet. She had to stay with her mother until she was six weeks old. Baby potbellied pigs are called piglets. Newborn piglets weigh 4 to 8 ounces (113 to 227 grams). Newborns spend most of their time drinking milk from their mother. Piglets are ready to be weaned around five to six weeks of age. By seven weeks of age, piglets are ready to go to a new home.

Pages 8–9

My pet potbellied pig was full grown after six months. She is about the size of a dog. After six months, piglets lose their baby teeth and grow adult teeth. Potbellied pigs are full-grown by two years of age. On average, potbellied pigs are about 16 inches (41 centimeters) tall and weigh about 100 pounds (45 kilograms).

Pages 10–11

My pet potbellied pig has a very big belly. Her belly touches the ground. A swayed back and a large, round belly are two of the most visible differences between potbellied pigs and farm pigs. The potbellied pig's back bends downward, pushing the belly closer to the ground. Sometimes, the belly is so large that it drags on the ground.

My pet potbellied pig has two long teeth called tusks. Her tusks are empty on the inside. Like other pig species, potbellied pigs grow tusks. Males grow larger tusks than females. Some pet owners prefer to get their potbellied pig's tusks trimmed. It is best to get this done by a veterinarian to ensure the safety of the pig.

My pet potbellied pig needs to eat twice each day. It is my job to make sure she gets the right amount of food. Potbellied pigs need to eat special food made just for miniature pigs. Potbellied pigs under three months old can eat as much as they want. After three months, their meal portions need to be watched closely to make sure they do not overeat.

My pet potbellied pig sleeps on her own bed. She also has her own litter box. Potbellied pigs need a bed to sleep on. Large dog beds work well. The bed should be placed in a quiet and warm part of the house. They also need a litter box. The box should be big enough for the pig to turn around in, with an opening no higher than 3 inches (8 cm) so the pig can get in and out easily.

My pet potbellied pig likes to be very clean. It is my job to bathe her, brush her, and clean her teeth. Potbellied pigs like to be clean. When they get dirty, they need a bath with special soap made for pigs. To clean your pig's teeth, use a damp cloth with baking soda. This should be done a few times each week.

I make sure my pet potbellied pig is healthy. I love my pet potbellied pig. Potbellied pigs need plenty of attention and exercise to stay healthy and happy. They like to go for walks, play fetch, and go swimming. It is a good idea to keep a child's wading pool so the pig can stay cool on hot days. Potbellied pigs have to visit a veterinarian for vaccinations and yearly checkups.

KEY WORDS

Research has shown that as much as 65 percent of all written material published in English is made up of 300 words. These 300 words cannot be taught using pictures or learned by sounding them out. They must be recognized by sight. This book contains 51 common sight words to help young readers improve their reading fluency and comprehension. This book also teaches young readers several important content words, such as proper nouns. These words are paired with pictures to aid in learning and improve understanding.

Page	Sight Words First Appearance
4	good, her, I, my, of, take
6	a, had, mother, old, she, to, until, was, with
9	about, after, can, grown, is, the, up
11	big, has, very
12	are, called, have, larger, long, on, than, two
15	all, day, each, eat, food, gets, it, keep, make, needs, right, their, will
16	also, own
18	and, be, likes

Page	Content Words First Appearance
4	care, pet, potbellied pig
6	piglet, weeks
9	dog, months, pounds, size
11	belly, ground
12	females, inside, male, teeth, tusks
15	amount, job
16	bed, litter box
18	sunscreen
21	healthy

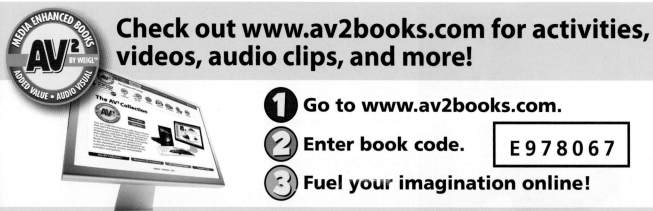